The best pet

Sam and his pal Asher are running a pet contest. Some pets will win ribbons and the best pet will win a cup.

2

There are lots of pets entered
in the contest. Nan has her
hens with her and Miss Good
has her cat, Fluff.

Miss Good is brushing Fluff's coat. She says, "You are the best pet for me."

Sam and Asher look at all
the pets one by one. They
discuss the pets and then
they think hard.

Sid wins the green ribbon for
the pet that can sleep in all
spots. Sid grins and naps.

Gus wins the red ribbon for munching on tops and socks. He is spoiling a pair of socks with his teeth.

Nan's hens get top spot for clucking. The hens' wings clap and the hens cluck!

Pam wins the number one ribbon for the pet with the biggest bark. Pam wags her tail and barks.

Tim's pup, Fizz, wins the brown ribbon for the pet with lots of spots! He creeps into Tim's lap and yaps.

Meg's rabbit, Mack, wins
a ribbon for the pet with
the softest fur. Mack
crunches on a carrot.

Miss Good's black cat, Fluff, gets the cup for best pet. She licks herself and grins.

Sid sits up. He snarls and
growls. He is mad!

Sid runs at Fluff! Fluff speeds off. Pam jumps up and runs at Sid. Fizz yaps and runs with Pam.

The hens hop up into the
air and there are a lot of
flapping wings. Gus and
Mack join in too!

Sam and Asher get the number one ribbon for the best ruckus at a pet contest!

Words to blend

contest	Fluff	brushing
best	spots	naps
clucking	munching	clap
cluck	longest	softest
crunches	black	herself
grins	jumps	flapping
carrot	ruckus	ribbon

Before reading

Synopsis: Sam and Asher are organising a pet competition. Will there be prizes for all the pets – Fluff, Mack, Sid, Pam, Fizz, Gus and Nan's hens?

Review graphemes/phonemes: ee ow ar oi

Story discussion: Look at the cover and read the title together. Ask: *What do you think is happening in the picture? If there was a pet contest between the different pets in this series, who do you think would win?*

Link to prior learning: Display a word with adjacent consonants from the story, e.g. *spoiling*. Ask the children to put a dot under the single-letter graphemes (*s, p, l, i*) and a line under the digraphs (*oi, ng*). Model, if necessary, how to sound out and blend the sounds together to read the word. Repeat with another word from the story, e.g. *growls*, and encourage the children to sound out and blend the word independently.

Vocabulary check: snarls – growls with bared teeth

Decoding practice: Display the following words: *snarls, sleep, free, brown, cluck, softest*. See how quickly children can read the words. Encourage them to read without overtly sounding out and blending if possible, but remind them to sound out and blend if they get stuck.

Tricky word practice: Display the word *one* and explain that in this word, the /w/ and /o/ sounds are made by *o*, and the /n/ sound is made by *ne*. Practise writing and reading the word.

After reading

Apply learning: Ask: *Do you think the pet contest was successful? Why, or why not?*

Comprehension

- Who decides to have a pet contest?

- Which pets enter the contest?

- Do you think Fluff deserved to win the cup for best pet?

Fluency

- Pick a page that most of the group read quite easily. Ask them to reread it with pace and expression. Model how to do this if necessary.

- Ask children to choose a favourite page and read it with lots of appropriate expression.

- Practise reading the words on page 17.

Tricky words review

some	are	there
do	you	little
all	by	they
she	me	he
says	I	oh